The Calendar

How Long Is a MONTH?

by Claire Clark
Consulting Editor: Gail Saunders-Smith, PhD

CAPSTONE PRESS
a capstone imprint

Pebble Plus is published by Capstone Press,
1710 Roe Crest Drive, North Mankato, Minnesota 56003.
www.capstonepub.com

Books published by Capstone Press are manufactured with paper containing at least 10 percent post-consumer waste.

Library of Congress Cataloging-in-Publication Data
Clark, Claire, 1973–
How long is a month? / by Claire Clark.
p. cm. — (Pebble plus. The calendar)
Summary: "Simple text and photos explain a month as a unit of time and the months in a year"—Provided by publisher.
Includes bibliographical references and index.
ISBN 978-1-4296-7593-2 (library binding)
ISBN 978-1-4296-7899-5 (paperback)
1. Months—Juvenile literature. 2. Moon—Rotation—Juvenile literature. 3. Time measurements—Juvenile literature. I. Title. II. Series.

QB209.5.C5834 2012
529'.2—dc23 2011025046

Editorial Credits
Kristen Mohn, editor; Bobbie Nuytten, designer; Marcie Spence, media researcher; Sarah Schuette, photo stylist; Marcy Morin, studio scheduler; Kathy McColley, production specialist

Photo Credits
Capstone Studio: Amber Ross, 19, Karon Dubke, cover (girl), 5, 9 (bottom), 13, 15, 17, 21; Photodisc, 7; Shutterstock: Evgeni Stefanov, 11, Petr Vaclavek, cover (paper), Smit, 9 (top), Tom T Takai, cover (calendar), 1

Note to Parents and Teachers

The Calendar series supports national science and social studies standards related to time. This book describes and illustrates what makes a month. The images support early readers in understanding the text. The repetition of words and phrases helps early readers learn new words. This book also introduces early readers to subject-specific vocabulary words, which are defined in the Glossary section. Early readers may need assistance to read some words and to use the Table of Contents, Glossary, Read More, Internet Sites, and Index sections of the book.

Printed in the United States of America in North Mankato, Minnesota.
102011 006405CGS12

Table of Contents

What Is a Month?

Each month the ice cream shop has a new flavor. A month has between 28 and 31 days. July has 31 days of cherry swirl ice cream!

Raspberry
Speciality Flavour
Green Apple
Coconut
Mint
Flavor of the Month

Months have about 28 days
because of the moon.
The moon takes about
four weeks, or 28 days,
to travel once around Earth.

moon
Earth

Months of the Year

Twelve months equal one year.

A calendar shows the months.

The first month is January.

Next are February and March.

These are winter months.

JANUARY
Sunday
Monday
Tuesday
Wednesday
Thursday
Friday
Saturday
1
2
3
4
5
6
7
8
9
10
11
12
13
14
15
16
17
18
21
22

In April spring begins.
People plant flowers.
Squirrels come out of their
dens. In May frogs wake.
In June school's out.

It's summer!

In July and August

families camp and play.

In September

school starts again.

In October it's fall.

The weather cools.

November is a busy month.

Thanksgiving comes.

December means winter break!

What Happens in a Month?

In a month you grow.

Your hair grows a half-inch!

A seed sprouts into a plant.

Months can measure age.
A baby is one month old.
In 11 months he'll have
his first birthday.

At the ice cream shop

a month has passed.

Time for a new flavor!

In August it's bubble gum.

What kind do you like?

SADDLE RANCH

Glossary

calendar—a chart that shows all of the days, weeks, and months in a year

den—a place where a wild animal may live

flavor—the kind of taste in a food

measure—to find out the size of something

sprout—to start to grow

Read More

Mitten, Luana K. *My Calendar: Months of the Year.* Concepts. Vero Beach, Fla.: Rourke Pub., 2009.

Scheunemann, Pam. *Time to Learn about Weeks & Months.* Time. Edina, Minn.: ABDO Pub., 2008.

Steffora, Tracey. *Months of the Year.* Measuring Time. Chicago: Heinemann Library, 2011.

Internet Sites

FactHound offers a safe, fun way to find Internet sites related to this book. All of the sites on FactHound have been researched by our staff.

Here's all you do:

Visit *www.facthound.com*

Type in this code: 9781429675932

Check out projects, games and lots more at
www.capstonekids.com

Index

Word Count: 186
Grade: 1
Early-Intervention Level: 19